PLANNER

This Planner Belongs To

_____

ROUTINE

OUTINE

UTINE

Year At A Glance

JANUARY	**FEBRUARY**	**MARCH**
APRIL	**MAY**	**JUNE**
JULY	**AUGUST**	**SEPTEMBER**
OCTOBER	**NOVEMBER**	**DECEMBER**

Yearly Goals

	GOALS
CAREER	
FINANCIAL	
SPIRITUAL	
FITNESS	
RELATIONSHIP	

Important Days

January

February

March

April

May

June

July

August

September

October

November

December

Important Dates

WHAT?	WHEN?	WHERE?

NOTES

Birthdays To Remember

January

February

March

April

May

June

July

August

September

October

November

December

Monthly Planner

MONDAY	TUESDAY	WEDNESDAY	THURSDAY	FRIDAY	SATURDAY	SUNDAY

APPOINTMENTS

-
-
-
-
-

MONTHLY GOALS

-
-
-
-
-

Weekly Checklist

MONDAY

- [ ]
- [ ]
- [ ]
- [ ]
- [ ]

TUESDAY

- [ ]
- [ ]
- [ ]
- [ ]
- [ ]

WEDNESDAY

- [ ]
- [ ]
- [ ]
- [ ]
- [ ]

THURSDAY

- [ ]
- [ ]
- [ ]
- [ ]
- [ ]

FRIDAY

- [ ]
- [ ]
- [ ]
- [ ]
- [ ]

SATURDAY

- [ ]
- [ ]
- [ ]
- [ ]
- [ ]

SUNDAY

- [ ]
- [ ]
- [ ]
- [ ]
- [ ]

NOTES

Weekly Checklist

MONTH:

WEEK NUMBER:

MONDAY

- [ ]
- [ ]
- [ ]
- [ ]
- [ ]

TUESDAY

- [ ]
- [ ]
- [ ]
- [ ]
- [ ]

WEDNESDAY

- [ ]
- [ ]
- [ ]
- [ ]
- [ ]

THURSDAY

- [ ]
- [ ]
- [ ]
- [ ]
- [ ]

FRIDAY

- [ ]
- [ ]
- [ ]
- [ ]
- [ ]

SATURDAY

- [ ]
- [ ]
- [ ]
- [ ]
- [ ]

SUNDAY

- [ ]
- [ ]
- [ ]
- [ ]
- [ ]

NOTES

Weekly Checklist

MONTH:

WEEK NUMBER:

MONDAY
☑
☑
☑
☑
☑

TUESDAY
☑
☑
☑
☑
☑

WEDNESDAY
☑
☑
☑
☑
☑

THURSDAY
☑
☑
☑
☑
☑

FRIDAY
☑
☑
☑
☑
☑

SATURDAY
☑
☑
☑
☑
☑

SUNDAY
☑
☑
☑
☑
☑

NOTES

Weekly Checklist

MONTH:

WEEK NUMBER:

MONDAY
☑
☑
☑
☑
☑

TUESDAY
☑
☑
☑
☑
☑

WEDNESDAY
☑
☑
☑
☑
☑

THURSDAY
☑
☑
☑
☑
☑

FRIDAY
☑
☑
☑
☑
☑

SATURDAY
☑
☑
☑
☑

SUNDAY
☑
☑
☑
☑
☑

NOTES

Monthly Planner

MONTH OF:

MONDAY	TUESDAY	WEDNESDAY	THURSDAY	FRIDAY	SATURDAY	SUNDAY

APPOINTMENTS

MONTHLY GOALS

Weekly Checklist

MONTH:

WEEK NUMBER:

MONDAY
- [ ]
- [ ]
- [ ]
- [ ]
- [ ]

TUESDAY
- [ ]
- [ ]
- [ ]
- [ ]
- [ ]

WEDNESDAY
- [ ]
- [ ]
- [ ]
- [ ]
- [ ]

THURSDAY
- [ ]
- [ ]
- [ ]
- [ ]
- [ ]

FRIDAY
- [ ]
- [ ]
- [ ]
- [ ]
- [ ]

SATURDAY
- [ ]
- [ ]
- [ ]
- [ ]
- [ ]

SUNDAY
- [ ]
- [ ]
- [ ]
- [ ]
- [ ]

NOTES

Weekly Checklist

MONTH:

WEEK NUMBER:

MONDAY
☑
☑
☑
☑
☑

TUESDAY
☑
☑
☑
☑
☑

WEDNESDAY
☑
☑
☑
☑
☑

THURSDAY
☑
☑
☑
☑
☑

FRIDAY
☑
☑
☑
☑
☑

SATURDAY
☑
☑
☑
☑
☑

SUNDAY
☑
☑
☑
☑
☑

NOTES

Weekly Checklist

MONTH:

WEEK NUMBER:

MONDAY
- ☑
- ☑
- ☑
- ☑
- ☑

TUESDAY
- ☑
- ☑
- ☑
- ☑
- ☑

WEDNESDAY
- ☑
- ☑
- ☑
- ☑
- ☑

THURSDAY
- ☑
- ☑
- ☑
- ☑
- ☑

FRIDAY
- ☑
- ☑
- ☑
- ☑
- ☑

SATURDAY
- ☑
- ☑
- ☑
- ☑
- ☑

SUNDAY
- ☑
- ☑
- ☑
- ☑
- ☑

NOTES

Weekly Checklist

MONTH:

WEEK NUMBER:

MONDAY
☑
☑
☑
☑
☑

TUESDAY
☑
☑
☑
☑
☑

WEDNESDAY
☑
☑
☑
☑
☑

THURSDAY
☑
☑
☑
☑
☑

FRIDAY
☑
☑
☑
☑
☑

SATURDAY
☑
☑
☑
☑
☑

SUNDAY
☑
☑
☑
☑
☑

NOTES

Monthly Planner

MONTH OF:

MONDAY	TUESDAY	WEDNESDAY	THURSDAY	FRIDAY	SATURDAY	SUNDAY

APPOINTMENTS

MONTHLY GOALS

Weekly Checklist

MONDAY

- [x]
- [x]
- [x]
- [x]
- [x]

TUESDAY

- [x]
- [x]
- [x]
- [x]
- [x]

WEDNESDAY

- [x]
- [x]
- [x]
- [x]
- [x]

THURSDAY

- [x]
- [x]
- [x]
- [x]
- [x]

FRIDAY

- [x]
- [x]
- [x]
- [x]
- [x]

SATURDAY

- [x]
- [x]
- [x]
- [x]
- [x]

SUNDAY

- [x]
- [x]
- [x]
- [x]
- [x]

NOTES

Weekly Checklist

MONTH:

WEEK NUMBER:

MONDAY

- ☑
- ☑
- ☑
- ☑
- ☑

TUESDAY

- ☑
- ☑
- ☑
- ☑
- ☑

WEDNESDAY

- ☑
- ☑
- ☑
- ☑
- ☑

THURSDAY

- ☑
- ☑
- ☑
- ☑
- ☑

FRIDAY

- ☑
- ☑
- ☑
- ☑
- ☑

SATURDAY

- ☑
- ☑
- ☑
- ☑
- ☑

SUNDAY

- ☑
- ☑
- ☑
- ☑
- ☑

NOTES

Weekly Checklist

MONDAY
☑
☑
☑
☑
☑

TUESDAY
☑
☑
☑
☑
☑

WEDNESDAY
☑
☑
☑
☑
☑

THURSDAY
☑
☑
☑
☑
☑

FRIDAY
☑
☑
☑
☑
☑

SATURDAY
☑
☑
☑
☑
☑

SUNDAY
☑
☑
☑
☑
☑

NOTES

Weekly Checklist

MONTH:

WEEK NUMBER:

MONDAY
- [ ]
- [ ]
- [ ]
- [ ]
- [ ]

TUESDAY
- [ ]
- [ ]
- [ ]
- [ ]
- [ ]

WEDNESDAY
- [ ]
- [ ]
- [ ]
- [ ]
- [ ]

THURSDAY
- [ ]
- [ ]
- [ ]
- [ ]
- [ ]

FRIDAY
- [ ]
- [ ]
- [ ]
- [ ]
- [ ]

SATURDAY
- [ ]
- [ ]
- [ ]
- [ ]
- [ ]

SUNDAY
- [ ]
- [ ]
- [ ]
- [ ]
- [ ]

NOTES

Monthly Planner

MONDAY	TUESDAY	WEDNESDAY	THURSDAY	FRIDAY	SATURDAY	SUNDAY

APPOINTMENTS

MONTHLY GOALS

Weekly Checklist

MONTH:

WEEK NUMBER:

MONDAY

- ☑
- ☑
- ☑
- ☑
- ☑

TUESDAY

- ☑
- ☑
- ☑
- ☑
- ☑

WEDNESDAY

- ☑
- ☑
- ☑
- ☑
- ☑

THURSDAY

- ☑
- ☑
- ☑
- ☑
- ☑

FRIDAY

- ☑
- ☑
- ☑
- ☑
- ☑

SATURDAY

- ☑
- ☑
- ☑
- ☑
- ☑

SUNDAY

- ☑
- ☑
- ☑
- ☑
- ☑

NOTES

Weekly Checklist

MONTH:

WEEK NUMBER:

MONDAY
- ☑
- ☑
- ☑
- ☑
- ☑

TUESDAY
- ☑
- ☑
- ☑
- ☑
- ☑

WEDNESDAY
- ☑
- ☑
- ☑
- ☑
- ☑

THURSDAY
- ☑
- ☑
- ☑
- ☑
- ☑

FRIDAY
- ☑
- ☑
- ☑
- ☑
- ☑

SATURDAY
- ☑
- ☑
- ☑
- ☑
- ☑

SUNDAY
- ☑
- ☑
- ☑
- ☑
- ☑

NOTES

Weekly Checklist

MONTH:

WEEK NUMBER:

MONDAY
- [✓]
- [✓]
- [✓]
- [✓]
- [✓]

TUESDAY
- [✓]
- [✓]
- [✓]
- [✓]
- [✓]

WEDNESDAY
- [✓]
- [✓]
- [✓]
- [✓]
- [✓]

THURSDAY
- [✓]
- [✓]
- [✓]
- [✓]
- [✓]

FRIDAY
- [✓]
- [✓]
- [✓]
- [✓]
- [✓]

SATURDAY
- [✓]
- [✓]
- [✓]
- [✓]
- [✓]

SUNDAY
- [✓]
- [✓]
- [✓]
- [✓]
- [✓]

NOTES

Weekly Checklist

MONTH: **WEEK NUMBER:**

MONDAY	TUESDAY	WEDNESDAY
☑	☑	☑
☑	☑	☑
☑	☑	☑
☑	☑	☑
☑	☑	☑

THURSDAY	FRIDAY	SATURDAY
☑	☑	☑
☑	☑	☑
☑	☑	☑
☑	☑	☑
☑	☑	☑

SUNDAY	NOTES
☑	
☑	
☑	
☑	
☑	

Monthly Planner

MONDAY	TUESDAY	WEDNESDAY	THURSDAY	FRIDAY	SATURDAY	SUNDAY

APPOINTMENTS

MONTHLY GOALS

Weekly Checklist

MONTH:

WEEK NUMBER:

MONDAY	TUESDAY	WEDNESDAY
☑	☑	☑
☑	☑	☑
☑	☑	☑
☑	☑	☑
☑	☑	☑

THURSDAY	FRIDAY	SATURDAY
☑	☑	☑
☑	☑	☑
☑	☑	☑
☑	☑	☑
☑	☑	☑

SUNDAY	NOTES
☑	
☑	
☑	
☑	
☑	

Weekly Checklist

MONTH:

WEEK NUMBER:

MONDAY
- ☑
- ☑
- ☑
- ☑
- ☑

TUESDAY
- ☑
- ☑
- ☑
- ☑
- ☑

WEDNESDAY
- ☑
- ☑
- ☑
- ☑
- ☑

THURSDAY
- ☑
- ☑
- ☑
- ☑
- ☑

FRIDAY
- ☑
- ☑
- ☑
- ☑
- ☑

SATURDAY
- ☑
- ☑
- ☑
- ☑
- ☑

SUNDAY
- ☑
- ☑
- ☑
- ☑
- ☑

NOTES

Weekly Checklist

MONDAY

- [ ]
- [ ]
- [ ]
- [ ]
- [ ]

TUESDAY

- [ ]
- [ ]
- [ ]
- [ ]
- [ ]

WEDNESDAY

- [ ]
- [ ]
- [ ]
- [ ]
- [ ]

THURSDAY

- [ ]
- [ ]
- [ ]
- [ ]
- [ ]

FRIDAY

- [ ]
- [ ]
- [ ]
- [ ]
- [ ]

SATURDAY

- [ ]
- [ ]
- [ ]
- [ ]
- [ ]

SUNDAY

- [ ]
- [ ]
- [ ]
- [ ]
- [ ]

NOTES

Weekly Checklist

MONTH:

WEEK NUMBER:

MONDAY
- ☑
- ☑
- ☑
- ☑
- ☑

TUESDAY
- ☑
- ☑
- ☑
- ☑
- ☑

WEDNESDAY
- ☑
- ☑
- ☑
- ☑
- ☑

THURSDAY
- ☑
- ☑
- ☑
- ☑
- ☑

FRIDAY
- ☑
- ☑
- ☑
- ☑
- ☑

SATURDAY
- ☑
- ☑
- ☑
- ☑
- ☑

SUNDAY
- ☑
- ☑
- ☑
- ☑
- ☑

NOTES

Monthly Planner

MONTH OF:

MONDAY	TUESDAY	WEDNESDAY	THURSDAY	FRIDAY	SATURDAY	SUNDAY

Appointments

Monthly Goals

Weekly Checklist

MONTH:

WEEK NUMBER:

MONDAY
☑
☑
☑
☑
☑

TUESDAY
☑
☑
☑
☑
☑

WEDNESDAY
☑
☑
☑
☑
☑

THURSDAY
☑
☑
☑
☑
☑

FRIDAY
☑
☑
☑
☑
☑

SATURDAY
☑
☑
☑
☑
☑

SUNDAY
☑
☑
☑
☑
☑

NOTES

Weekly Checklist

MONTH:

WEEK NUMBER:

MONDAY

- [ ]
- [ ]
- [ ]
- [ ]
- [ ]

TUESDAY

- [ ]
- [ ]
- [ ]
- [ ]
- [ ]

WEDNESDAY

- [ ]
- [ ]
- [ ]
- [ ]
- [ ]

THURSDAY

- [ ]
- [ ]
- [ ]
- [ ]
- [ ]

FRIDAY

- [ ]
- [ ]
- [ ]
- [ ]
- [ ]

SATURDAY

- [ ]
- [ ]
- [ ]
- [ ]
- [ ]

SUNDAY

- [ ]
- [ ]
- [ ]
- [ ]
- [ ]

NOTES

Weekly Checklist

MONDAY
☑
☑
☑
☑
☑

TUESDAY
☑
☑
☑
☑
☑

WEDNESDAY
☑
☑
☑
☑
☑

THURSDAY
☑
☑
☑
☑
☑

FRIDAY
☑
☑
☑
☑
☑

SATURDAY
☑
☑
☑
☑
☑

SUNDAY
☑
☑
☑
☑
☑

NOTES

Weekly Checklist

MONTH: **WEEK NUMBER:**

MONDAY	TUESDAY	WEDNESDAY
☑	☑	☑
☑	☑	☑
☑	☑	☑
☑	☑	☑
☑	☑	☑

THURSDAY	FRIDAY	SATURDAY
☑	☑	☑
☑	☑	☑
☑	☑	☑
☑	☑	☑
☑	☑	☑

SUNDAY	NOTES
☑	
☑	
☑	
☑	
☑	

Monthly Planner

MONTH OF:

MONDAY	TUESDAY	WEDNESDAY	THURSDAY	FRIDAY	SATURDAY	SUNDAY

APPOINTMENTS

MONTHLY GOALS

Weekly Checklist

MONDAY
☑
☑
☑
☑
☑

TUESDAY
☑
☑
☑
☑
☑

WEDNESDAY
☑
☑
☑
☑
☑

THURSDAY
☑
☑
☑
☑
☑

FRIDAY
☑
☑
☑
☑
☑

SATURDAY
☑
☑
☑
☑
☑

SUNDAY
☑
☑
☑
☑
☑

NOTES

Weekly Checklist

MONTH:

WEEK NUMBER:

MONDAY
- [ ]
- [ ]
- [ ]
- [ ]
- [ ]

TUESDAY
- [ ]
- [ ]
- [ ]
- [ ]
- [ ]

WEDNESDAY
- [ ]
- [ ]
- [ ]
- [ ]
- [ ]

THURSDAY
- [ ]
- [ ]
- [ ]
- [ ]
- [ ]

FRIDAY
- [ ]
- [ ]
- [ ]
- [ ]
- [ ]

SATURDAY
- [ ]
- [ ]
- [ ]
- [ ]
- [ ]

SUNDAY
- [ ]
- [ ]
- [ ]
- [ ]
- [ ]

NOTES

Weekly Checklist

MONTH:　　　　　　　　　　　　**WEEK NUMBER:**

MONDAY
☑
☑
☑
☑
☑

TUESDAY
☑
☑
☑
☑
☑

WEDNESDAY
☑
☑
☑
☑
☑

THURSDAY
☑
☑
☑
☑
☑

FRIDAY
☑
☑
☑
☑
☑

SATURDAY
☑
☑
☑
☑
☑

SUNDAY
☑
☑
☑
☑
☑

NOTES

Weekly Checklist

MONTH: **WEEK NUMBER:**

MONDAY
☑
☑
☑
☑
☑

TUESDAY
☑
☑
☑
☑
☑

WEDNESDAY
☑
☑
☑
☑
☑

THURSDAY
☑
☑
☑
☑
☑

FRIDAY
☑
☑
☑
☑
☑

SATURDAY
☑
☑
☑
☑

SUNDAY
☑
☑
☑
☑
☑

NOTES

Monthly Planner

MONTH OF:

MONDAY	TUESDAY	WEDNESDAY	THURSDAY	FRIDAY	SATURDAY	SUNDAY

APPOINTMENTS

MONTHLY GOALS

Weekly Checklist

MONDAY

- [ ]
- [ ]
- [ ]
- [ ]
- [ ]

TUESDAY

- [ ]
- [ ]
- [ ]
- [ ]
- [ ]

WEDNESDAY

- [ ]
- [ ]
- [ ]
- [ ]
- [ ]

THURSDAY

- [ ]
- [ ]
- [ ]
- [ ]
- [ ]

FRIDAY

- [ ]
- [ ]
- [ ]
- [ ]
- [ ]

SATURDAY

- [ ]
- [ ]
- [ ]
- [ ]
- [ ]

SUNDAY

- [ ]
- [ ]
- [ ]
- [ ]
- [ ]

NOTES

Weekly Checklist

WEEK NUMBER:

MONDAY
- ☑
- ☑
- ☑
- ☑
- ☑

TUESDAY
- ☑
- ☑
- ☑
- ☑
- ☑

WEDNESDAY
- ☑
- ☑
- ☑
- ☑
- ☑

THURSDAY
- ☑
- ☑
- ☑
- ☑
- ☑

FRIDAY
- ☑
- ☑
- ☑
- ☑
- ☑

SATURDAY
- ☑
- ☑
- ☑
- ☑
- ☑

SUNDAY
- ☑
- ☑
- ☑
- ☑
- ☑

NOTES

Weekly Checklist

MONTH:

WEEK NUMBER:

MONDAY
☑
☑
☑
☑
☑

TUESDAY
☑
☑
☑
☑
☑

WEDNESDAY
☑
☑
☑
☑
☑

THURSDAY
☑
☑
☑
☑
☑

FRIDAY
☑
☑
☑
☑
☑

SATURDAY
☑
☑
☑
☑
☑

SUNDAY
☑
☑
☑
☑
☑

NOTES

Weekly Checklist

MONTH:

WEEK NUMBER:

MONDAY
- ☑
- ☑
- ☑
- ☑
- ☑

TUESDAY
- ☑
- ☑
- ☑
- ☑
- ☑

WEDNESDAY
- ☑
- ☑
- ☑
- ☑
- ☑

THURSDAY
- ☑
- ☑
- ☑
- ☑
- ☑

FRIDAY
- ☑
- ☑
- ☑
- ☑
- ☑

SATURDAY
- ☑
- ☑
- ☑
- ☑
- ☑

SUNDAY
- ☑
- ☑
- ☑
- ☑
- ☑

NOTES

Monthly Planner

MONDAY	TUESDAY	WEDNESDAY	THURSDAY	FRIDAY	SATURDAY	SUNDAY

APPOINTMENTS

-
-
-
-
-

MONTHLY GOALS

-
-
-
-
-

Weekly Checklist

MONTH:　　　　　　　　　　**WEEK NUMBER:**

MONDAY
- ☑
- ☑
- ☑
- ☑
- ☑

TUESDAY
- ☑
- ☑
- ☑
- ☑
- ☑

WEDNESDAY
- ☑
- ☑
- ☑
- ☑
- ☑

THURSDAY
- ☑
- ☑
- ☑
- ☑
- ☑

FRIDAY
- ☑
- ☑
- ☑
- ☑
- ☑

SATURDAY
- ☑
- ☑
- ☑
- ☑
- ☑

SUNDAY
- ☑
- ☑
- ☑
- ☑
- ☑

NOTES

Weekly Checklist

MONDAY

- [ ]
- [ ]
- [ ]
- [ ]
- [ ]

TUESDAY

- [ ]
- [ ]
- [ ]
- [ ]
- [ ]

WEDNESDAY

- [ ]
- [ ]
- [ ]
- [ ]
- [ ]

THURSDAY

- [ ]
- [ ]
- [ ]
- [ ]
- [ ]

FRIDAY

- [ ]
- [ ]
- [ ]
- [ ]
- [ ]

SATURDAY

- [ ]
- [ ]
- [ ]
- [ ]
- [ ]

SUNDAY

- [ ]
- [ ]
- [ ]
- [ ]
- [ ]

NOTES

Weekly Checklist

MONTH: **WEEK NUMBER:**

MONDAY
- ☑
- ☑
- ☑
- ☑
- ☑

TUESDAY
- ☑
- ☑
- ☑
- ☑
- ☑

WEDNESDAY
- ☑
- ☑
- ☑
- ☑
- ☑

THURSDAY
- ☑
- ☑
- ☑
- ☑
- ☑

FRIDAY
- ☑
- ☑
- ☑
- ☑
- ☑

SATURDAY
- ☑
- ☑
- ☑
- ☑
- ☑

SUNDAY
- ☑
- ☑
- ☑
- ☑
- ☑

NOTES

Weekly Checklist

MONTH:

WEEK NUMBER:

MONDAY
☑
☑
☑
☑
☑

TUESDAY
☑
☑
☑
☑
☑

WEDNESDAY
☑
☑
☑
☑
☑

THURSDAY
☑
☑
☑
☑
☑

FRIDAY
☑
☑
☑
☑
☑

SATURDAY
☑
☑
☑
☑
☑

SUNDAY
☑
☑
☑
☑
☑

NOTES

Monthly Planner

MONDAY	TUESDAY	WEDNESDAY	THURSDAY	FRIDAY	SATURDAY	SUNDAY

APPOINTMENTS

-
-
-
-
-

MONTHLY GOALS

-
-
-
-
-

Weekly Checklist

MONTH: **WEEK NUMBER:**

MONDAY
- [ ]
- [ ]
- [ ]
- [ ]
- [ ]

TUESDAY
- [ ]
- [ ]
- [ ]
- [ ]
- [ ]

WEDNESDAY
- [ ]
- [ ]
- [ ]
- [ ]
- [ ]

THURSDAY
- [ ]
- [ ]
- [ ]
- [ ]
- [ ]

FRIDAY
- [ ]
- [ ]
- [ ]
- [ ]
- [ ]

SATURDAY
- [ ]
- [ ]
- [ ]
- [ ]
- [ ]

SUNDAY
- [ ]
- [ ]
- [ ]
- [ ]
- [ ]

NOTES

Weekly Checklist

MONTH: **WEEK NUMBER:**

MONDAY
- [ ]
- [ ]
- [ ]
- [ ]
- [ ]

TUESDAY
- [ ]
- [ ]
- [ ]
- [ ]
- [ ]

WEDNESDAY
- [ ]
- [ ]
- [ ]
- [ ]
- [ ]

THURSDAY
- [ ]
- [ ]
- [ ]
- [ ]
- [ ]

FRIDAY
- [ ]
- [ ]
- [ ]
- [ ]
- [ ]

SATURDAY
- [ ]
- [ ]
- [ ]
- [ ]
- [ ]

SUNDAY
- [ ]
- [ ]
- [ ]
- [ ]
- [ ]

NOTES

Weekly Checklist

MONDAY
- [ ]
- [ ]
- [ ]
- [ ]
- [ ]

TUESDAY
- [ ]
- [ ]
- [ ]
- [ ]
- [ ]

WEDNESDAY
- [ ]
- [ ]
- [ ]
- [ ]
- [ ]

THURSDAY
- [ ]
- [ ]
- [ ]
- [ ]
- [ ]

FRIDAY
- [ ]
- [ ]
- [ ]
- [ ]
- [ ]

SATURDAY
- [ ]
- [ ]
- [ ]
- [ ]
- [ ]

SUNDAY
- [ ]
- [ ]
- [ ]
- [ ]
- [ ]

NOTES

Weekly Checklist

MONTH: **WEEK NUMBER:**

MONDAY	TUESDAY	WEDNESDAY
☑	☑	☑
☑	☑	☑
☑	☑	☑
☑	☑	☑
☑	☑	☑

THURSDAY	FRIDAY	SATURDAY
☑	☑	☑
☑	☑	☑
☑	☑	☑
☑	☑	☑
☑	☑	☑

SUNDAY	NOTES
☑	
☑	
☑	
☑	
☑	

Monthly Planner

MONDAY	TUESDAY	WEDNESDAY	THURSDAY	FRIDAY	SATURDAY	SUNDAY

APPOINTMENTS

MONTHLY GOALS

Weekly Checklist

WEEK NUMBER:

MONDAY
- ☑
- ☑
- ☑
- ☑
- ☑

TUESDAY
- ☑
- ☑
- ☑
- ☑
- ☑

WEDNESDAY
- ☑
- ☑
- ☑
- ☑
- ☑

THURSDAY
- ☑
- ☑
- ☑
- ☑
- ☑

FRIDAY
- ☑
- ☑
- ☑
- ☑
- ☑

SATURDAY
- ☑
- ☑
- ☑
- ☑
- ☑

SUNDAY
- ☑
- ☑
- ☑
- ☑
- ☑

NOTES

Weekly Checklist

MONTH:

WEEK NUMBER:

MONDAY
- ☑
- ☑
- ☑
- ☑
- ☑

TUESDAY
- ☑
- ☑
- ☑
- ☑
- ☑

WEDNESDAY
- ☑
- ☑
- ☑
- ☑
- ☑

THURSDAY
- ☑
- ☑
- ☑
- ☑
- ☑

FRIDAY
- ☑
- ☑
- ☑
- ☑
- ☑

SATURDAY
- ☑
- ☑
- ☑
- ☑
- ☑

SUNDAY
- ☑
- ☑
- ☑
- ☑
- ☑

NOTES

Weekly Checklist

MONTH: **WEEK NUMBER:**

MONDAY	TUESDAY	WEDNESDAY
☑	☑	☑
☑	☑	☑
☑	☑	☑
☑	☑	☑
☑	☑	☑

THURSDAY	FRIDAY	SATURDAY
☑	☑	☑
☑	☑	☑
☑	☑	☑
☑	☑	☑
☑	☑	☑

SUNDAY	NOTES
☑	
☑	
☑	
☑	
☑	

Weekly Checklist

MONTH:　　　　　　　　　　　　　　　　**WEEK NUMBER:**

MONDAY
☑
☑
☑
☑
☑

TUESDAY
☑
☑
☑
☑
☑

WEDNESDAY
☑
☑
☑
☑
☑

THURSDAY
☑
☑
☑
☑
☑

FRIDAY
☑
☑
☑
☑
☑

SATURDAY
☑
☑
☑
☑
☑

SUNDAY
☑
☑
☑
☑
☑

NOTES

Monthly Planner

MONTH OF:

MONDAY	TUESDAY	WEDNESDAY	THURSDAY	FRIDAY	SATURDAY	SUNDAY

APPOINTMENTS

MONTHLY GOALS

Weekly Checklist

MONTH:

WEEK NUMBER:

MONDAY
- [ ]
- [ ]
- [ ]
- [ ]
- [ ]

TUESDAY
- [ ]
- [ ]
- [ ]
- [ ]
- [ ]

WEDNESDAY
- [ ]
- [ ]
- [ ]
- [ ]
- [ ]

THURSDAY
- [ ]
- [ ]
- [ ]
- [ ]
- [ ]

FRIDAY
- [ ]
- [ ]
- [ ]
- [ ]
- [ ]

SATURDAY
- [ ]
- [ ]
- [ ]
- [ ]
- [ ]

SUNDAY
- [ ]
- [ ]
- [ ]
- [ ]
- [ ]

NOTES

Weekly Checklist

MONDAY

- ☑
- ☑
- ☑
- ☑
- ☑

TUESDAY

- ☑
- ☑
- ☑
- ☑
- ☑

WEDNESDAY

- ☑
- ☑
- ☑
- ☑
- ☑

THURSDAY

- ☑
- ☑
- ☑
- ☑
- ☑

FRIDAY

- ☑
- ☑
- ☑
- ☑
- ☑

SATURDAY

- ☑
- ☑
- ☑
- ☑
- ☑

SUNDAY

- ☑
- ☑
- ☑
- ☑
- ☑

NOTES

Weekly Checklist

MONTH:

WEEK NUMBER:

MONDAY
☑
☑
☑
☑
☑

TUESDAY
☑
☑
☑
☑
☑

WEDNESDAY
☑
☑
☑
☑
☑

THURSDAY
☑
☑
☑
☑
☑

FRIDAY
☑
☑
☑
☑
☑

SATURDAY
☑
☑
☑
☑
☑

SUNDAY
☑
☑
☑
☑
☑

NOTES

Weekly Checklist

MONDAY
☑
☑
☑
☑
☑

TUESDAY
☑
☑
☑
☑
☑

WEDNESDAY
☑
☑
☑
☑
☑

THURSDAY
☑
☑
☑
☑
☑

FRIDAY
☑
☑
☑
☑
☑

SATURDAY
☑
☑
☑
☑
☑

SUNDAY
☑
☑
☑
☑
☑

NOTES

HOUSEHOLD

Household & Services

ELECTRIC
ELECTRIC PROVIDER
ACCOUNT NUMBER
RENEWAL DATE
PHONE NUMBER

GAS
GAS PROVIDER
ACCOUNT NUMBER
RENEWAL DATE
PHONE NUMBER

WATER
WATER PROVIDER
ACCOUNT NUMBER
RENEWAL DATE
PHONE NUMBER

INTERNET
INTERNET PROVIDER
ACCOUNT NUMBER
RENEWAL DATE
PHONE NUMBER

CABLE
CABLE PROVIDER
ACCOUNT NUMBER
RENEWAL DATE
PHONE NUMBER

SEWER
SEWER PROVIDER
ACCOUNT NUMBER
RENEWAL DATE
PHONE NUMBER

Grocery List

DATE:

☐
☐
☐
☐
☐

☐
☐
☐
☐
☐

☐
☐
☐
☐
☐

☐
☐
☐
☐
☐

☐
☐
☐
☐
☐

☐
☐
☐
☐
☐

☐
☐
☐
☐
☐

☐
☐
☐
☐
☐

☐
☐
☐
☐
☐

Grocery List

DATE:

☐
☐
☐
☐
☐

☐
☐
☐
☐
☐

☐
☐
☐
☐
☐

Monthly Meal Planner

MONTH: _____

WEEK 1	THU: _____
MON: _____	FRI: _____
TUE: _____	SAT: _____
WED: _____	SUN: _____

WEEK 2	THU: _____
MON: _____	FRI: _____
TUE: _____	SAT: _____
WED: _____	SUN: _____

WEEK 3	THU: _____
MON: _____	FRI: _____
TUE: _____	SAT: _____
WED: _____	SUN: _____

WEEK 4	THU: _____
MON: _____	FRI: _____
TUE: _____	SAT: _____
WED: _____	SUN: _____

Monthly Meal Planner

MONTH: _____

WEEK 1	
	THU: _____
MON: _____	FRI: _____
TUE: _____	SAT: _____
WED: _____	SUN: _____

WEEK 2	
	THU: _____
MON: _____	FRI: _____
TUE: _____	SAT: _____
WED: _____	SUN: _____

WEEK 3	
	THU: _____
MON: _____	FRI: _____
TUE: _____	SAT: _____
WED: _____	SUN: _____

WEEK 4	
	THU: _____
MON: _____	FRI: _____
TUE: _____	SAT: _____
WED: _____	SUN: _____

Monthly Meal Planner

MONTH: _____

WEEK 1

THU: _____

MON: _____ FRI: _____

TUE: _____ SAT: _____

WED: _____ SUN: _____

WEEK 2

THU: _____

MON: _____ FRI: _____

TUE: _____ SAT: _____

WED: _____ SUN: _____

WEEK 3

THU: _____

MON: _____ FRI: _____

TUE: _____ SAT: _____

WED: _____ SUN: _____

WEEK 4

THU: _____

MON: _____ FRI: _____

TUE: _____ SAT: _____

WED: _____ SUN: _____

Monthly Meal Planner

MONTH: _____

WEEK 1

MON: _____
TUE: _____
WED: _____

THU: _____
FRI: _____
SAT: _____
SUN: _____

WEEK 2

MON: _____
TUE: _____
WED: _____

THU: _____
FRI: _____
SAT: _____
SUN: _____

WEEK 3

MON: _____
TUE: _____
WED: _____

THU: _____
FRI: _____
SAT: _____
SUN: _____

WEEK 4

MON: _____
TUE: _____
WED: _____

THU: _____
FRI: _____
SAT: _____
SUN: _____

Monthly Meal Planner

MONTH: _____

WEEK 1	THU: _____
MON: _____	FRI: _____
TUE: _____	SAT: _____
WED: _____	SUN: _____

WEEK 2	THU: _____
MON: _____	FRI: _____
TUE: _____	SAT: _____
WED: _____	SUN: _____

WEEK 3	THU: _____
MON: _____	FRI: _____
TUE: _____	SAT: _____
WED: _____	SUN: _____

WEEK 4	THU: _____
MON: _____	FRI: _____
TUE: _____	SAT: _____
WED: _____	SUN: _____

Monthly Meal Planner

MONTH: _____

WEEK 1

MON: _____

TUE: _____

WED: _____

THU: _____

FRI: _____

SAT: _____

SUN: _____

WEEK 2

MON: _____

TUE: _____

WED: _____

THU: _____

FRI: _____

SAT: _____

SUN: _____

WEEK 3

MON: _____

TUE: _____

WED: _____

THU: _____

FRI: _____

SAT: _____

SUN: _____

WEEK 4

MON: _____

TUE: _____

WED: _____

THU: _____

FRI: _____

SAT: _____

SUN: _____

Monthly Meal Planner

MONTH: _____

WEEK 1

MON: _____

TUE: _____

WED: _____

THU: _____

FRI: _____

SAT: _____

SUN: _____

WEEK 2

MON: _____

TUE: _____

WED: _____

THU: _____

FRI: _____

SAT: _____

SUN: _____

WEEK 3

MON: _____

TUE: _____

WED: _____

THU: _____

FRI: _____

SAT: _____

SUN: _____

WEEK 4

MON: _____

TUE: _____

WED: _____

THU: _____

FRI: _____

SAT: _____

SUN: _____

Monthly Meal Planner

MONTH: _____

WEEK 1

THU: _____

MON: _____ FRI: _____

TUE: _____ SAT: _____

WED: _____ SUN: _____

WEEK 2

THU: _____

MON: _____ FRI: _____

TUE: _____ SAT: _____

WED: _____ SUN: _____

WEEK 3

THU: _____

MON: _____ FRI: _____

TUE: _____ SAT: _____

WED: _____ SUN: _____

WEEK 4

THU: _____

MON: _____ FRI: _____

TUE: _____ SAT: _____

WED: _____ SUN: _____

Monthly Meal Planner

MONTH: _____

WEEK 1

MON: _____
TUE: _____
WED: _____
THU: _____
FRI: _____
SAT: _____
SUN: _____

WEEK 2

MON: _____
TUE: _____
WED: _____
THU: _____
FRI: _____
SAT: _____
SUN: _____

WEEK 3

MON: _____
TUE: _____
WED: _____
THU: _____
FRI: _____
SAT: _____
SUN: _____

WEEK 4

MON: _____
TUE: _____
WED: _____
THU: _____
FRI: _____
SAT: _____
SUN: _____

Monthly Meal Planner

MONTH:

WEEK 1

THU: _____

MON: _____   FRI: _____

TUE: _____   SAT: _____

WED: _____   SUN: _____

WEEK 2

THU: _____

MON: _____   FRI: _____

TUE: _____   SAT: _____

WED: _____   SUN: _____

WEEK 3

THU: _____

MON: _____   FRI: _____

TUE: _____   SAT: _____

WED: _____   SUN: _____

WEEK 4

THU: _____

MON: _____   FRI: _____

TUE: _____   SAT: _____

WED: _____   SUN: _____

Monthly Meal Planner

MONTH: _____

WEEK 1

MON: _____ THU: _____

TUE: _____ FRI: _____

WED: _____ SAT: _____

_____ SUN: _____

WEEK 2

MON: _____ THU: _____

TUE: _____ FRI: _____

WED: _____ SAT: _____

_____ SUN: _____

WEEK 3

MON: _____ THU: _____

TUE: _____ FRI: _____

WED: _____ SAT: _____

_____ SUN: _____

WEEK 4

MON: _____ THU: _____

TUE: _____ FRI: _____

WED: _____ SAT: _____

_____ SUN: _____

Monthly Meal Planner

MONTH: _____

WEEK 1

MON: _____

TUE: _____

WED: _____

THU: _____

FRI: _____

SAT: _____

SUN: _____

WEEK 2

MON: _____

TUE: _____

WED: _____

THU: _____

FRI: _____

SAT: _____

SUN: _____

WEEK 3

MON: _____

TUE: _____

WED: _____

THU: _____

FRI: _____

SAT: _____

SUN: _____

WEEK 4

MON: _____

TUE: _____

WED: _____

THU: _____

FRI: _____

SAT: _____

SUN: _____

Car Maintenance

Date	Repairs/Checks	Mileage	Repair Shop	Cost

Password Tracker

WEBSITE URL	
USERNAME	
PASSWORD	
E-MAIL	
NOTES	

WEBSITE URL	
USERNAME	
PASSWORD	
E-MAIL	
NOTES	

WEBSITE URL	
USERNAME	
PASSWORD	
E-MAIL	
NOTES	

WEBSITE URL	
USERNAME	
PASSWORD	
E-MAIL	
NOTES	

WEBSITE URL	
USERNAME	
PASSWORD	
E-MAIL	
NOTES	

WEBSITE URL	
USERNAME	
PASSWORD	
E-MAIL	
NOTES	

WEBSITE URL	
USERNAME	
PASSWORD	
E-MAIL	
NOTES	

WEBSITE URL	
USERNAME	
PASSWORD	
E-MAIL	
NOTES	

Password Tracker

WEBSITE URL	
USERNAME	
PASSWORD	
E-MAIL	
NOTES	

WEBSITE URL	
USERNAME	
PASSWORD	
E-MAIL	
NOTES	

WEBSITE URL	
USERNAME	
PASSWORD	
E-MAIL	
NOTES	

WEBSITE URL	
USERNAME	
PASSWORD	
E-MAIL	
NOTES	

WEBSITE URL	
USERNAME	
PASSWORD	
E-MAIL	
NOTES	

WEBSITE URL	
USERNAME	
PASSWORD	
E-MAIL	
NOTES	

WEBSITE URL	
USERNAME	
PASSWORD	
E-MAIL	
NOTES	

WEBSITE URL	
USERNAME	
PASSWORD	
E-MAIL	
NOTES	

Subscriptions Tracker

SUBSCRIPTION	COST	FREQUENCY	RENEWAL DATE
		☐ MONTHLY ☐ ANNUALLY	
		☐ MONTHLY ☐ ANNUALLY	
		☐ MONTHLY ☐ ANNUALLY	
		☐ MONTHLY ☐ ANNUALLY	
		☐ MONTHLY ☐ ANNUALLY	
		☐ MONTHLY ☐ ANNUALLY	
		☐ MONTHLY ☐ ANNUALLY	
		☐ MONTHLY ☐ ANNUALLY	
		☐ MONTHLY ☐ ANNUALLY	
		☐ MONTHLY ☐ ANNUALLY	
		☐ MONTHLY ☐ ANNUALLY	
		☐ MONTHLY ☐ ANNUALLY	

Subscriptions Tracker

SUBSCRIPTION	COST	FREQUENCY	RENEWAL DATE
		☐ MONTHLY ☐ ANNUALLY	
		☐ MONTHLY ☐ ANNUALLY	
		☐ MONTHLY ☐ ANNUALLY	
		☐ MONTHLY ☐ ANNUALLY	
		☐ MONTHLY ☐ ANNUALLY	
		☐ MONTHLY ☐ ANNUALLY	
		☐ MONTHLY ☐ ANNUALLY	
		☐ MONTHLY ☐ ANNUALLY	
		☐ MONTHLY ☐ ANNUALLY	
		☐ MONTHLY ☐ ANNUALLY	
		☐ MONTHLY ☐ ANNUALLY	
		☐ MONTHLY ☐ ANNUALLY	

Important Contact List

NAME	
PHONE	
E-MAIL	
ADDRESS	

NAME	
PHONE	
E-MAIL	
ADDRESS	

NAME	
PHONE	
E-MAIL	
ADDRESS	

NAME	
PHONE	
E-MAIL	
ADDRESS	

NAME	
PHONE	
E-MAIL	
ADDRESS	

NAME	
PHONE	
E-MAIL	
ADDRESS	

NAME	
PHONE	
E-MAIL	
ADDRESS	

NAME	
PHONE	
E-MAIL	
ADDRESS	

Important Contact List

NAME	
PHONE	
E-MAIL	
ADDRESS	

NAME	
PHONE	
E-MAIL	
ADDRESS	

NAME	
PHONE	
E-MAIL	
ADDRESS	

NAME	
PHONE	
E-MAIL	
ADDRESS	

NAME	
PHONE	
E-MAIL	
ADDRESS	

NAME	
PHONE	
E-MAIL	
ADDRESS	

NAME	
PHONE	
E-MAIL	
ADDRESS	

NAME	
PHONE	
E-MAIL	
ADDRESS	

Online Purchase Tracker

DATE	PRODUCTS	WEBSITE	EST. ARRIVAL	COST	RECEIVED
					☐
					☐
					☐
					☐
					☐
					☐
					☐
					☐
					☐
					☐
					☐
					☐
					☐
					☐
					☐
					☐
					☐
					☐
					☐
					☐
					☐
					☐
					☐

Online Purchase Tracker

DATE	PRODUCTS	WEBSITE	EST. ARRIVAL	COST	RECEIVED
					☐
					☐
					☐
					☐
					☐
					☐
					☐
					☐
					☐
					☐
					☐
					☐
					☐
					☐
					☐
					☐
					☐
					☐
					☐
					☐
					☐
					☐

Cleaning Schedule

January

February

March

April

May

June

July

August

September

October

November

December

SELF-CARE

Yearly Mood Tracker

YEAR:

DATE	JAN	FEB	MAR	APR	MAY	JUN	JUL	AUG	SEP	OCT	NOV	DEC
1												
2												
3												
4												
5												
6												
7												
8												
9												
10												
11												
12												
13												
14												
15												
16												
17												
18												
19												
20												
21												
22												
23												
24												
25												
26												
27												
28												
29												
30												
31												

COLOR CODES

My Motivation

DATE:

My Affirmation

Today I'm Thankful For

Daily Vision

What's On My Mind

Daily Goals

Today I'm Excited About

Goal Setter

JAN	FEB	MAR	APR	MAY	JUN

JUL	AUG	SEP	OCT	NOV	DEC

HOME

FINANCE

HEALTH

RELATIONSHIP

FITNESS

STUDY

Goal Breakdown

GOAL:

START DATE:

ACHIEVE GOAL BY:

PLAN

_____

_____

_____

_____

_____

STEPS

DEADLINE

1): _____ ☐ _____

2): _____ ☐ _____

3): _____ ☐ _____

4): _____ ☐ _____

5): _____ ☐ _____

NOTES & IDEAS

Books To Read

NAME OF THE BOOK	AUTHOR

1) _____   _____

2) _____   _____

3) _____   _____

4) _____   _____

5) _____   _____

6) _____   _____

7) _____   _____

8) _____   _____

9) _____   _____

10) _____   _____

11) _____   _____

12) _____   _____

13) _____   _____

14) _____   _____

15) _____   _____

NOTES

Habit Tracker

MONTH:

1	2	3	4	5	6	7	8	9	10
11	12	13	14	15	16	17	18	19	20
21	22	23	24	25	26	27	28	29	30
31									

HABIT

1	2	3	4	5	6	7	8	9	10
11	12	13	14	15	16	17	18	19	20
21	22	23	24	25	26	27	28	29	30
31									

HABIT

1	2	3	4	5	6	7	8	9	10
11	12	13	14	15	16	17	18	19	20
21	22	23	24	25	26	27	28	29	30
31									

HABIT

1	2	3	4	5	6	7	8	9	10
11	12	13	14	15	16	17	18	19	20
21	22	23	24	25	26	27	28	29	30
31									

HABIT

1	2	3	4	5	6	7	8	9	10
11	12	13	14	15	16	17	18	19	20
21	22	23	24	25	26	27	28	29	30
31									

HABIT

1	2	3	4	5	6	7	8	9	10
11	12	13	14	15	16	17	18	19	20
21	22	23	24	25	26	27	28	29	30
31									

HABIT

1	2	3	4	5	6	7	8	9	10
11	12	13	14	15	16	17	18	19	20
21	22	23	24	25	26	27	28	29	30
31									

HABIT

1	2	3	4	5	6	7	8	9	10
11	12	13	14	15	16	17	18	19	20
21	22	23	24	25	26	27	28	29	30
31									

HABIT

Habit Tracker

MONTH:

1	2	3	4	5	6	7	8	9	10
11	12	13	14	15	16	17	18	19	20
21	22	23	24	25	26	27	28	29	30
31									
HABIT									

1	2	3	4	5	6	7	8	9	10
11	12	13	14	15	16	17	18	19	20
21	22	23	24	25	26	27	28	29	30
31									
HABIT									

1	2	3	4	5	6	7	8	9	10
11	12	13	14	15	16	17	18	19	20
21	22	23	24	25	26	27	28	29	30
31									
HABIT									

1	2	3	4	5	6	7	8	9	10
11	12	13	14	15	16	17	18	19	20
21	22	23	24	25	26	27	28	29	30
31									
HABIT									

1	2	3	4	5	6	7	8	9	10
11	12	13	14	15	16	17	18	19	20
21	22	23	24	25	26	27	28	29	30
31									
HABIT									

1	2	3	4	5	6	7	8	9	10
11	12	13	14	15	16	17	18	19	20
21	22	23	24	25	26	27	28	29	30
31									
HABIT									

1	2	3	4	5	6	7	8	9	10
11	12	13	14	15	16	17	18	19	20
21	22	23	24	25	26	27	28	29	30
31									
HABIT									

1	2	3	4	5	6	7	8	9	10
11	12	13	14	15	16	17	18	19	20
21	22	23	24	25	26	27	28	29	30
31									
HABIT									

Doctor Visits Log

DATE	DOCTOR	REASON	NOTES	FOLLOW UP

Medication Tracker

DATE	TIME	MEDICINE	PURPOSE	DOSE

Medication Tracker

DATE	TIME	MEDICINE	PURPOSE	DOSE

Daily self-assessment log

Week Of									
Month	Year								
	S	M	T	W	T	F	S	Notes	
Felt Productive									
Felt Joy									
Felt Afraid									
Felt Proud									
Felt Loved									
Felt Happy									
Felt Mad									
Felt Anxiety									
Cried									
Laughed Out Loud									
Went For A Walk									
Enjoyed A Meal									
Prepared A Meal									
Had Very Dark Thoughts									
Had A Panic Attack									
Read For Pleasure									
Did Laundry									
Watched TV (# of hrs)									
Exercised									
Socialized									

Week Of									
Month	Year								
	S	M	T	W	T	F	S	Notes	
Felt Productive									
Felt Joy									
Felt Afraid									
Felt Proud									
Felt Loved									
Felt Happy									
Felt Mad									
Felt Anxiety									
Cried									
Laughed Out Loud									
Went For A Walk									
Enjoyed A Meal									
Prepared A Meal									
Had Very Dark Thoughts									
Had A Panic Attack									
Read For Pleasure									
Did Laundry									
Watched TV (# of hrs)									
Exercised									
Socialized									

Daily self-assessment log

Week Of									
Month	Year								
	S	M	T	W	T	F	S	Notes
Felt Productive									
Felt Joy									
Felt Afraid									
Felt Proud									
Felt Loved									
Felt Happy									
Felt Mad									
Felt Anxiety									
Cried									
Laughed Out Loud									
Went For A Walk									
Enjoyed A Meal									
Prepared A Meal									
Had Very Dark Thoughts									
Had A Panic Attack									
Read For Pleasure									
Did Laundry									
Watched TV (# of hrs)									
Exercised									
Socialized									

Week Of									
Month	Year								
	S	M	T	W	T	F	S	Notes
Felt Productive									
Felt Joy									
Felt Afraid									
Felt Proud									
Felt Loved									
Felt Happy									
Felt Mad									
Felt Anxiety									
Cried									
Laughed Out Loud									
Went For A Walk									
Enjoyed A Meal									
Prepared A Meal									
Had Very Dark Thoughts									
Had A Panic Attack									
Read For Pleasure									
Did Laundry									
Watched TV (# of hrs)									
Exercised									
Socialized									

Daily self-assessment log

Week Of									
Month		Year							
	S	M	T	W	T	F	S	Notes	
Felt Productive									
Felt Joy									
Felt Afraid									
Felt Proud									
Felt Loved									
Felt Happy									
Felt Mad									
Felt Anxiety									
Cried									
Laughed Out Loud									
Went For A Walk									
Enjoyed A Meal									
Prepared A Meal									
Had Very Dark Thoughts									
Had A Panic Attack									
Read For Pleasure									
Did Laundry									
Watched TV (# of hrs)									
Exercised									
Socialized									

Week Of									
Month		Year							
	S	M	T	W	T	F	S	Notes	
Felt Productive									
Felt Joy									
Felt Afraid									
Felt Proud									
Felt Loved									
Felt Happy									
Felt Mad									
Felt Anxiety									
Cried									
Laughed Out Loud									
Went For A Walk									
Enjoyed A Meal									
Prepared A Meal									
Had Very Dark Thoughts									
Had A Panic Attack									
Read For Pleasure									
Did Laundry									
Watched TV (# of hrs)									
Exercised									
Socialized									

Daily self-assessment log

Week Of										
Month	Year									
		S	M	T	W	T	F	S	Notes
Felt Productive										
Felt Joy										
Felt Afraid										
Felt Proud										
Felt Loved										
Felt Happy										
Felt Mad										
Felt Anxiety										
Cried										
Laughed Out Loud										
Went For A Walk										
Enjoyed A Meal										
Prepared A Meal										
Had Very Dark Thoughts										
Had A Panic Attack										
Read For Pleasure										
Did Laundry										
Watched TV (# of hrs)										
Exercised										
Socialized										

Week Of										
Month	Year									
		S	M	T	W	T	F	S	Notes
Felt Productive										
Felt Joy										
Felt Afraid										
Felt Proud										
Felt Loved										
Felt Happy										
Felt Mad										
Felt Anxiety										
Cried										
Laughed Out Loud										
Went For A Walk										
Enjoyed A Meal										
Prepared A Meal										
Had Very Dark Thoughts										
Had A Panic Attack										
Read For Pleasure										
Did Laundry										
Watched TV (# of hrs)										
Exercised										
Socialized										

Daily self-assessment log

Week Of									
Month	Year								
	S	M	T	W	T	F	S	Notes	
Felt Productive									
Felt Joy									
Felt Afraid									
Felt Proud									
Felt Loved									
Felt Happy									
Felt Mad									
Felt Anxiety									
Cried									
Laughed Out Loud									
Went For A Walk									
Enjoyed A Meal									
Prepared A Meal									
Had Very Dark Thoughts									
Had A Panic Attack									
Read For Pleasure									
Did Laundry									
Watched TV (# of hrs)									
Exercised									
Socialized									

Week Of									
Month	Year								
	S	M	T	W	T	F	S	Notes	
Felt Productive									
Felt Joy									
Felt Afraid									
Felt Proud									
Felt Loved									
Felt Happy									
Felt Mad									
Felt Anxiety									
Cried									
Laughed Out Loud									
Went For A Walk									
Enjoyed A Meal									
Prepared A Meal									
Had Very Dark Thoughts									
Had A Panic Attack									
Read For Pleasure									
Did Laundry									
Watched TV (# of hrs)									
Exercised									
Socialized									

Daily self-assessment log

Week Of									
Month	Year								
	S	M	T	W	T	F	S	Notes
Felt Productive									
Felt Joy									
Felt Afraid									
Felt Proud									
Felt Loved									
Felt Happy									
Felt Mad									
Felt Anxiety									
Cried									
Laughed Out Loud									
Went For A Walk									
Enjoyed A Meal									
Prepared A Meal									
Had Very Dark Thoughts									
Had A Panic Attack									
Read For Pleasure									
Did Laundry									
Watched TV (# of hrs)									
Exercised									
Socialized									

Week Of									
Month	Year								
	S	M	T	W	T	F	S	Notes
Felt Productive									
Felt Joy									
Felt Afraid									
Felt Proud									
Felt Loved									
Felt Happy									
Felt Mad									
Felt Anxiety									
Cried									
Laughed Out Loud									
Went For A Walk									
Enjoyed A Meal									
Prepared A Meal									
Had Very Dark Thoughts									
Had A Panic Attack									
Read For Pleasure									
Did Laundry									
Watched TV (# of hrs)									
Exercised									
Socialized									

Daily self-assessment log

Week Of									
Month Year									
	S	M	T	W	T	F	S	Notes
Felt Productive									
Felt Joy									
Felt Afraid									
Felt Proud									
Felt Loved									
Felt Happy									
Felt Mad									
Felt Anxiety									
Cried									
Laughed Out Loud									
Went For A Walk									
Enjoyed A Meal									
Prepared A Meal									
Had Very Dark Thoughts									
Had A Panic Attack									
Read For Pleasure									
Did Laundry									
Watched TV (# of hrs)									
Exercised									
Socialized									

Week Of									
Month Year									
	S	M	T	W	T	F	S	Notes
Felt Productive									
Felt Joy									
Felt Afraid									
Felt Proud									
Felt Loved									
Felt Happy									
Felt Mad									
Felt Anxiety									
Cried									
Laughed Out Loud									
Went For A Walk									
Enjoyed A Meal									
Prepared A Meal									
Had Very Dark Thoughts									
Had A Panic Attack									
Read For Pleasure									
Did Laundry									
Watched TV (# of hrs)									
Exercised									
Socialized									

Daily self-assessment log

Week Of Month Year	S	M	T	W	T	F	S	Notes
Felt Productive								
Felt Joy								
Felt Afraid								
Felt Proud								
Felt Loved								
Felt Happy								
Felt Mad								
Felt Anxiety								
Cried								
Laughed Out Loud								
Went For A Walk								
Enjoyed A Meal								
Prepared A Meal								
Had Very Dark Thoughts								
Had A Panic Attack								
Read For Pleasure								
Did Laundry								
Watched TV (# of hrs)								
Exercised								
Socialized								

Week Of Month Year	S	M	T	W	T	F	S	Notes
Felt Productive								
Felt Joy								
Felt Afraid								
Felt Proud								
Felt Loved								
Felt Happy								
Felt Mad								
Felt Anxiety								
Cried								
Laughed Out Loud								
Went For A Walk								
Enjoyed A Meal								
Prepared A Meal								
Had Very Dark Thoughts								
Had A Panic Attack								
Read For Pleasure								
Did Laundry								
Watched TV (# of hrs)								
Exercised								
Socialized								

Daily self-assessment log

Week Of									
Month	Year								
	S	M	T	W	T	F	S	Notes	
Felt Productive									
Felt Joy									
Felt Afraid									
Felt Proud									
Felt Loved									
Felt Happy									
Felt Mad									
Felt Anxiety									
Cried									
Laughed Out Loud									
Went For A Walk									
Enjoyed A Meal									
Prepared A Meal									
Had Very Dark Thoughts									
Had A Panic Attack									
Read For Pleasure									
Did Laundry									
Watched TV (# of hrs)									
Exercised									
Socialized									

Week Of									
Month	Year								
	S	M	T	W	T	F	S	Notes	
Felt Productive									
Felt Joy									
Felt Afraid									
Felt Proud									
Felt Loved									
Felt Happy									
Felt Mad									
Felt Anxiety									
Cried									
Laughed Out Loud									
Went For A Walk									
Enjoyed A Meal									
Prepared A Meal									
Had Very Dark Thoughts									
Had A Panic Attack									
Read For Pleasure									
Did Laundry									
Watched TV (# of hrs)									
Exercised									
Socialized									

Daily self-assessment log

Week Of									
Month	Year								
		S	M	T	W	T	F	S	Notes
Felt Productive									
Felt Joy									
Felt Afraid									
Felt Proud									
Felt Loved									
Felt Happy									
Felt Mad									
Felt Anxiety									
Cried									
Laughed Out Loud									
Went For A Walk									
Enjoyed A Meal									
Prepared A Meal									
Had Very Dark Thoughts									
Had A Panic Attack									
Read For Pleasure									
Did Laundry									
Watched TV (# of hrs)									
Exercised									
Socialized									

Week Of									
Month	Year								
		S	M	T	W	T	F	S	Notes
Felt Productive									
Felt Joy									
Felt Afraid									
Felt Proud									
Felt Loved									
Felt Happy									
Felt Mad									
Felt Anxiety									
Cried									
Laughed Out Loud									
Went For A Walk									
Enjoyed A Meal									
Prepared A Meal									
Had Very Dark Thoughts									
Had A Panic Attack									
Read For Pleasure									
Did Laundry									
Watched TV (# of hrs)									
Exercised									
Socialized									

Daily self-assessment log

Week Of									
Month	Year								
	S	M	T	W	T	F	S	Notes
Felt Productive									
Felt Joy									
Felt Afraid									
Felt Proud									
Felt Loved									
Felt Happy									
Felt Mad									
Felt Anxiety									
Cried									
Laughed Out Loud									
Went For A Walk									
Enjoyed A Meal									
Prepared A Meal									
Had Very Dark Thoughts									
Had A Panic Attack									
Read For Pleasure									
Did Laundry									
Watched TV (# of hrs)									
Exercised									
Socialized									

Week Of									
Month	Year								
	S	M	T	W	T	F	S	Notes
Felt Productive									
Felt Joy									
Felt Afraid									
Felt Proud									
Felt Loved									
Felt Happy									
Felt Mad									
Felt Anxiety									
Cried									
Laughed Out Loud									
Went For A Walk									
Enjoyed A Meal									
Prepared A Meal									
Had Very Dark Thoughts									
Had A Panic Attack									
Read For Pleasure									
Did Laundry									
Watched TV (# of hrs)									
Exercised									
Socialized									

Daily self-assessment log

Week Of									
Month	Year								
	S	M	T	W	T	F	S	Notes	
Felt Productive									
Felt Joy									
Felt Afraid									
Felt Proud									
Felt Loved									
Felt Happy									
Felt Mad									
Felt Anxiety									
Cried									
Laughed Out Loud									
Went For A Walk									
Enjoyed A Meal									
Prepared A Meal									
Had Very Dark Thoughts									
Had A Panic Attack									
Read For Pleasure									
Did Laundry									
Watched TV (# of hrs)									
Exercised									
Socialized									

Week Of									
Month	Year								
	S	M	T	W	T	F	S	Notes	
Felt Productive									
Felt Joy									
Felt Afraid									
Felt Proud									
Felt Loved									
Felt Happy									
Felt Mad									
Felt Anxiety									
Cried									
Laughed Out Loud									
Went For A Walk									
Enjoyed A Meal									
Prepared A Meal									
Had Very Dark Thoughts									
Had A Panic Attack									
Read For Pleasure									
Did Laundry									
Watched TV (# of hrs)									
Exercised									
Socialized									

Daily Sleep Log

		1	2	3	4	5	6	7	8	9	10	11	12	13	14	15	16	17	18	19	20	21	22	23	24	25	26	27	28	29	30	31
PM	7																															
	8																															
	10																															
	11																															
AM	12																															
	1																															
	2																															
	3																															
	4																															
	5																															
	6																															
	7																															
	8																															
	10																															
	11																															
PM	12																															
	1																															
	2																															
	3																															
	4																															
	5																															
	6																															

		1	2	3	4	5	6	7	8	9	10	11	12	13	14	15	16	17	18	19	20	21	22	23	24	25	26	27	28	29	30	31
PM	7																															
	8																															
	10																															
	11																															
AM	12																															
	1																															
	2																															
	3																															
	4																															
	5																															
	6																															
	7																															
	8																															
	9																															
	10																															
	11																															
PM	12																															
	1																															
	2																															
	3																															
	4																															
	5																															
	6																															

Daily Sleep Log

		1	2	3	4	5	6	7	8	9	10	11	12	13	14	15	16	17	18	19	20	21	22	23	24	25	26	27	28	29	30	31
PM	7																															
	8																															
	10																															
	11																															
AM	12																															
	1																															
	2																															
	3																															
	4																															
	5																															
	6																															
	7																															
	8																															
	9																															
	10																															
	11																															
PM	12																															
	1																															
	2																															
	3																															
	4																															
	5																															
	6																															

		1	2	3	4	5	6	7	8	9	10	11	12	13	14	15	16	17	18	19	20	21	22	23	24	25	26	27	28	29	30	31
PM	7																															
	8																															
	10																															
	11																															
AM	12																															
	1																															
	2																															
	3																															
	4																															
	5																															
	6																															
	7																															
	8																															
	9																															
	10																															
	11																															
PM	12																															
	1																															
	2																															
	3																															
	4																															
	5																															
	6																															

Daily Sleep Log

		1	2	3	4	5	6	7	8	9	10	11	12	13	14	15	16	17	18	19	20	21	22	23	24	25	26	27	28	29	30	31
PM	7																															
	8																															
	10																															
	11																															
AM	12																															
	1																															
	2																															
	3																															
	4																															
	5																															
	6																															
	7																															
	8																															
	9																															
	10																															
	11																															
PM	12																															
	1																															
	2																															
	3																															
	4																															
	5																															
	6																															

		1	2	3	4	5	6	7	8	9	10	11	12	13	14	15	16	17	18	19	20	21	22	23	24	25	26	27	28	29	30	31
PM	7																															
	8																															
	10																															
	11																															
AM	12																															
	1																															
	2																															
	3																															
	4																															
	5																															
	6																															
	7																															
	8																															
	9																															
	10																															
	11																															
PM	12																															
	1																															
	2																															
	3																															
	4																															
	5																															
	6																															

Daily Sleep Log

		1	2	3	4	5	6	7	8	9	10	11	12	13	14	15	16	17	18	19	20	21	22	23	24	25	26	27	28	29	30	31
PM	7																															
	8																															
	10																															
	11																															
AM	12																															
	1																															
	2																															
	3																															
	4																															
	5																															
	6																															
	7																															
	8																															
	9																															
	10																															
	11																															
PM	12																															
	1																															
	2																															
	3																															
	4																															
	5																															
	6																															

		1	2	3	4	5	6	7	8	9	10	11	12	13	14	15	16	17	18	19	20	21	22	23	24	25	26	27	28	29	30	31
PM	7																															
	8																															
	10																															
	11																															
AM	12																															
	1																															
	2																															
	3																															
	4																															
	5																															
	6																															
	7																															
	8																															
	9																															
	10																															
	11																															
PM	12																															
	1																															
	2																															
	3																															
	4																															
	5																															
	6																															

Daily Sleep Log

		1	2	3	4	5	6	7	8	9	10	11	12	13	14	15	16	17	18	19	20	21	22	23	24	25	26	27	28	29	30	31
PM	7																															
	8																															
	10																															
	11																															
AM	12																															
	1																															
	2																															
	3																															
	4																															
	5																															
	6																															
	7																															
	8																															
	9																															
	10																															
	11																															
PM	12																															
	1																															
	2																															
	3																															
	4																															
	5																															
	6																															

		1	2	3	4	5	6	7	8	9	10	11	12	13	14	15	16	17	18	19	20	21	22	23	24	25	26	27	28	29	30	31
PM	7																															
	8																															
	10																															
	11																															
AM	12																															
	1																															
	2																															
	3																															
	4																															
	5																															
	6																															
	7																															
	8																															
	9																															
	10																															
	11																															
PM	12																															
	1																															
	2																															
	3																															
	4																															
	5																															
	6																															

Daily Sleep Log

		1	2	3	4	5	6	7	8	9	10	11	12	13	14	15	16	17	18	19	20	21	22	23	24	25	26	27	28	29	30	31
PM	7																															
	8																															
	10																															
	11																															
AM	12																															
	1																															
	2																															
	3																															
	4																															
	5																															
	6																															
	7																															
	8																															
	9																															
	10																															
	11																															
PM	12																															
	1																															
	2																															
	3																															
	4																															
	5																															
	6																															

		1	2	3	4	5	6	7	8	9	10	11	12	13	14	15	16	17	18	19	20	21	22	23	24	25	26	27	28	29	30	31
PM	7																															
	8																															
	10																															
	11																															
AM	12																															
	1																															
	2																															
	3																															
	4																															
	5																															
	6																															
	7																															
	8																															
	9																															
	10																															
	11																															
PM	12																															
	1																															
	2																															
	3																															
	4																															
	5																															
	6																															

FITNESS

Fitness Goals

START DATE: **END DATE:**

GOALS

MOTIVATION

MY PLAN

BEFORE	AFTER

My Measurements

DATE:

BEFORE & AFTER

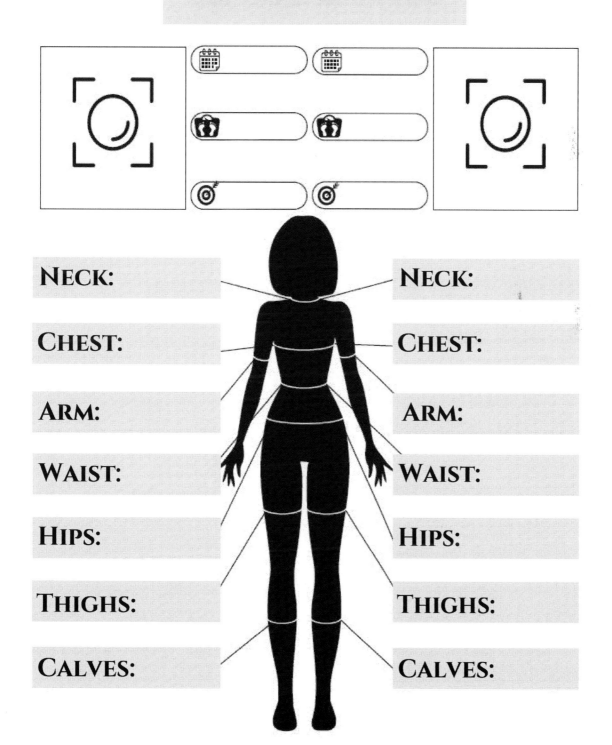

NECK:

NECK:

CHEST:

CHEST:

ARM:

ARM:

WAIST:

WAIST:

HIPS:

HIPS:

THIGHS:

THIGHS:

CALVES:

CALVES:

Weight Loss Tracker

DATE: **GOAL:**

WEEK1 _____	**WEEK 2** _____	**WEEK 3** _____	**WEEK 4** _____	**WEEK 5** _____
WEEK 6 _____	**WEEK 7** _____	**WEEK 8** _____	**WEEK 9** _____	**WEEK 10** _____
WEEK 11 _____	**WEEK 12** _____	**WEEK 13** _____	**WEEK 14** _____	**WEEK 15** _____
WEEK 16 _____	**WEEK 17** _____	**WEEK 18** _____	**WEEK 19** _____	**WEEK 20** _____
WEEK 21 _____	**WEEK 22** _____	**WEEK 23** _____	**WEEK 24** _____	**WEEK 25** _____
WEEK 26 _____	**WEEK 27** _____	**WEEK 28** _____	**WEEK 29** _____	**WEEK 30** _____

Weight Loss Tracker

DATE: _____ **GOAL:** _____

WEEK 1 _____	**WEEK 2** _____	**WEEK 3** _____	**WEEK 4** _____	**WEEK 5** _____
WEEK 6 _____	**WEEK 7** _____	**WEEK 8** _____	**WEEK 9** _____	**WEEK 10** _____
WEEK 11 _____	**WEEK 12** _____	**WEEK 13** _____	**WEEK 14** _____	**WEEK 15** _____
WEEK 16 _____	**WEEK 17** _____	**WEEK 18** _____	**WEEK 19** _____	**WEEK 20** _____
WEEK 21 _____	**WEEK 22** _____	**WEEK 23** _____	**WEEK 24** _____	**WEEK 25** _____
WEEK 26 _____	**WEEK 27** _____	**WEEK 28** _____	**WEEK 29** _____	**WEEK 30** _____

FINANCES

Monthly Budget

DATE	DESCRIPTION	AMOUNT	AFTER TAX

FIXED EXPENSES

DATE	DESCRIPTION	AMOUNT
	TOTAL	

OTHER EXPENSES

DATE	DESCRIPTION	AMOUNT
	TOTAL	

	GOAL	ACTUAL	DIFFERENCE
EARNT			
SPENT			
DEBT			
SAVED			

Monthly Budget

DATE	DESCRIPTION	AMOUNT	AFTER TAX

FIXED EXPENSES

DATE	DESCRIPTION	AMOUNT
	TOTAL	

OTHER EXPENSES

DATE	DESCRIPTION	AMOUNT
	TOTAL	

	GOAL	ACTUAL	DIFFERENCE
EARNT			
SPENT			
DEBT			
SAVED			

Monthly Budget

DATE	DESCRIPTION	AMOUNT	AFTER TAX

FIXED EXPENSES

DATE	DESCRIPTION	AMOUNT
	TOTAL	

OTHER EXPENSES

DATE	DESCRIPTION	AMOUNT
	TOTAL	

	GOAL	ACTUAL	DIFFERENCE
EARNT			
SPENT			
DEBT			
SAVED			

Monthly Budget

DATE	DESCRIPTION	AMOUNT	AFTER TAX

FIXED EXPENSES

DATE	DESCRIPTION	AMOUNT
	TOTAL	

OTHER EXPENSES

DATE	DESCRIPTION	AMOUNT
	TOTAL	

	GOAL	ACTUAL	DIFFERENCE
EARNT			
SPENT			
DEBT			
SAVED			

Monthly Budget

DATE	DESCRIPTION	AMOUNT	AFTER TAX

FIXED EXPENSES

DATE	DESCRIPTION	AMOUNT
	TOTAL	

OTHER EXPENSES

DATE	DESCRIPTION	AMOUNT
	TOTAL	

	GOAL	ACTUAL	DIFFERENCE
EARNT			
SPENT			
DEBT			
SAVED			

Monthly Budget

DATE	DESCRIPTION	AMOUNT	AFTER TAX

Fixed Expenses

DATE	DESCRIPTION	AMOUNT
	TOTAL	

Other Expenses

DATE	DESCRIPTION	AMOUNT
	TOTAL	

	GOAL	ACTUAL	DIFFERENCE
EARNT			
SPENT			
DEBT			
SAVED			

Monthly Budget

DATE	DESCRIPTION	AMOUNT	AFTER TAX

FIXED EXPENSES

DATE	DESCRIPTION	AMOUNT
	TOTAL	

OTHER EXPENSES

DATE	DESCRIPTION	AMOUNT
	TOTAL	

	GOAL	ACTUAL	DIFFERENCE
EARNT			
SPENT			
DEBT			
SAVED			

Monthly Budget

DATE	DESCRIPTION	AMOUNT	AFTER TAX

Fixed Expenses

DATE	DESCRIPTION	AMOUNT
	TOTAL	

Other Expenses

DATE	DESCRIPTION	AMOUNT
	TOTAL	

	GOAL	ACTUAL	DIFFERENCE
EARNT			
SPENT			
DEBT			
SAVED			

Monthly Budget

DATE	DESCRIPTION	AMOUNT	AFTER TAX

FIXED EXPENSES

DATE	DESCRIPTION	AMOUNT
	TOTAL	

OTHER EXPENSES

DATE	DESCRIPTION	AMOUNT
	TOTAL	

	GOAL	ACTUAL	DIFFERENCE
EARNT			
SPENT			
DEBT			
SAVED			

Monthly Budget

DATE	DESCRIPTION	AMOUNT	AFTER TAX

Fixed Expenses

DATE	DESCRIPTION	AMOUNT
	TOTAL	

Other Expenses

DATE	DESCRIPTION	AMOUNT
	TOTAL	

	GOAL	ACTUAL	DIFFERENCE
EARNT			
SPENT			
DEBT			
SAVED			

Monthly Budget

DATE	DESCRIPTION	AMOUNT	AFTER TAX

FIXED EXPENSES

DATE	DESCRIPTION	AMOUNT
	TOTAL	

OTHER EXPENSES

DATE	DESCRIPTION	AMOUNT
	TOTAL	

	GOAL	ACTUAL	DIFFERENCE
EARNT			
SPENT			
DEBT			
SAVED			

Monthly Budget

DATE	DESCRIPTION	AMOUNT	AFTER TAX

FIXED EXPENSES

DATE	DESCRIPTION	AMOUNT
	TOTAL	

OTHER EXPENSES

DATE	DESCRIPTION	AMOUNT
	TOTAL	

	GOAL	ACTUAL	DIFFERENCE
EARNT			
SPENT			
DEBT			
SAVED			

Debt Planner

CREDITOR	BALANCE	INTEREST RATE	MINIMUM PAYMENT	GOAL PAYMENT	PAID

Bill Tracker

MONTH: TOTAL:

BILL	AMOUNT	DUE DATE	PAID

Income Tracker

MONTH OF:

DATE	SOURCE	DESCRIPTION	AMOUNT
		TOTAL	

Expense Tracker

MONTH OF:

DATE	CATEGORY	DESCRIPTION	AMOUNT
		TOTAL	

My Savings

SAVING FOR	
AMOUNT	
DUE BY	

DEPOSITS

Printed in Great Britain
by Amazon